portfolio collection
Gerhardt Knodel

TELOS

Contents

above right:
Hush-Hsuh
1993
mixed media
10 x 10 x 9 in
(25 x 25 x 23cm)

illustration page 6:
Echo-oh
1993
mixed media
10 x 24 x 6 in
(25 x 61 x 15cm)

Travels with Silk

In the past I have travelled quite a lot. I've always kept a journal of experiences as one means for recreating the sense of environment remembered once I have returned home.

Years ago, on a trip around the world, in addition to my journal I took a three yard length of silk fabric with me. Along the way I anticipated opportunities for the silk fabric to interact with my experiences. The following notes are from my diary.

2/20   *I pressed the silk into the stone hand of David at Forest Lawn cemetery Los Angeles.*

3/1   *I blindfolded the statue of King Kamehameha on Kalakaua Blvd. in Honolulu.*

3/10   *In Kyoto I covered a bouquet of red carnations with the white silk.*

3/22   *Hong Kong. Went to the 19th floor of an apartment building and hung the fabric from an open window along with laundry hung by the residents from almost every other window in the building.*

3/29   *Bali. Placed the fabric around my shoulders and walked into the Indian Ocean.*

4/12	*India. Placed the fabric around my shoulders and walked into the Bay of Benghal.*
4/12	*India. Placed the fabric around my shoulders and walked into the Bay of Benghal.*
4/30	*Egypt. Climbed to the top of one of the great Pyramids and capped that Pyramid with my white silk.*
5/5	*Greece. On the hottest day of this year I tied a string to each corner and suspended the silk like a canopy between columns of the Parthenon.*
5/19	*Istanbul. Unrolled the fabric at the entrance to Constantine's Hagi-Sofia, and then walked on the fabric as I entered the Church, now a museum.*
6/8	*England. Entered Westminster Abbey. Unrolled the white silk on pew 84 covering the seat and back of the hard brown oak, and sat down.*
12/25	*I wrapped the base of my Christmas Tree with that same piece of white silk.*

Two years later, on the first day that I used my new studio, I laid the fabric at the entrance and walked over it to enter.

The white silk now hangs on a wall of my studio in Pontiac, Michigan, where most people see it as no more than a length of fabric. But I regard it as a resplendent mirror of its extraordinary experience and wonder what more it might be.

G K (1980)

The New Millennium

Of all the consequences of the stroke of the new millennium, none seems more potent than the redefinition of the moment itself. For the first time in history, millions of people and locations around the globe experience their stroke of midnight in relationship to one another. The source of joy in Sydney and then Delhi soon became the same source that ignited crowds in Berlin, then London. One's own midnight seemed extended on what preceded and followed. Each midnight seemed to frame time, creating a passage to the next, sustaining the moment like the resonance of a bell heard round the world.

If there is essential meaning in the birth of the 21st Century, it must exist within a concept of time as a container requiring 24 midnights to become filled. We now can move from self definition relative to focussed moments in time to the self that lives 24 hours simultaneously. Our 'befores' and our 'afters' may now be constantly with us expanding each moment of our days and our nights from local to global. The earth has moved from object to sensation as communication media have erased boundaries and distance revealing a new world with no impenetrable walls.

G K (2000)

Birdwall
1990
screen printed cotton
bonded with silk,
polypropylene net
96 x 180 x 12in
(240 x 450 x 30cm)

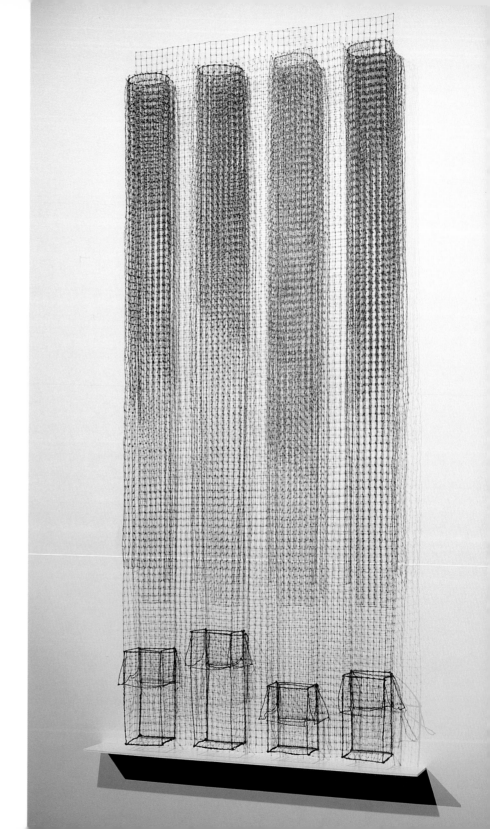

Summer Reign
1992
metallic foil, linen, cotton,
polypropylene net,
painted aluminium
30 x 72 x 5in (75 x 180 x 12cm)

Burnt Norton

Time present and time past
Are both perhaps present in time future,
And time future contained in time past.
If all time is eternally present
All time is unredeemable.
What might have been is an abstraction
Remaining a perpetual possibility
Only in a world of speculation.
What might have been and what has been
Point to one end, which is always present.
Footballs echo in the memory
Down the passage which we did not take
Toward the door we never opened
Into the rose garden.

T. S. Eliot

Gulf Stream
1977
wool, mylar, aluminium, steel
240 x 1200 x 360in (600 x 3000 x 900cm)
Anderson Library, University of Houston, Texas

above:

Parhelic Path

1975

mylar, rayon, cotton

240 x 100 x 96in

(600 x 100 x 240cm)

page 16:

Grand Exchange

1981

wool, mylar, metal, nylon

height: 624in (1560cm)

Cincinnati Bell of Ohio

right:

Free Fall

1977

mylar, wool, rayon, metal, acrylic

840 x 180 x 120in (2100 x 450 x 25cm)

Renaissance Centre, Detroit

Gerhardt Knodel: Inhabitations

by Marsha Miro

The physical origin of Gerhardt Knodel's work is in the grid—the basic structure of loom woven textiles and a universally used pattern of organization. While the grid locates his art within the textile medium and its historical evolution, it also links it to the phenomenon of centering. The intersection of horizontal and vertical, warp and weft, of longitude and latitude creates an internal order that has physical, cultural, social and architectural meaning used by Knodel in the work. Each intersection anticipates the next one and the next, "reflecting," writes Knodel, "the entire history of weaving as a recreation of the essence of textiles, an echo of that first moment of discovery in the construction of a textile. Each new intersection returns to that original moment and is a promise of that which is to come. To weave is to renew."[1]

Knodel uses the grid as a structural definition of the space into which he weaves his imagery. A series of woven textile planes suspended in space is configured to become another plane of fabric that stretches into space to make another space. The grid is the germinal form with which he builds a flat textile and then he constructs an architectural unit; a wall and the space inside that wall, a box and the place within Knodel's art is about the existential nature of confinement, within the structure of the grid, within a plane and a space

defined by textiles; further, within the human body, within pictorial and abstract images, and individual fantasies—the former three providing the place for considering and experiencing the latter. Textiles traditionally are fabricated containers. Clothing, tents, and tapestries are walls that shelter the body. Textiles in non-Western cultures and early cultures were valued as locus making, as a way of centering human beings, physically and metaphorically. While Knodel works site specifically, he also uses his installations to create an expressive context that transcends its physical characteristics. Like a stage set or the tent for a travelling circus, his constructions pull together elements that transform a space into a place with focused meaning. He does this by building relationships between the measure of a space and its conceptualization, between events and possibilities, the historical past and developing situations. *In Invisible Cities,* by Italo Calvino, a book Knodel admires, Calvino writes: "The city...does not tell its part, but contains it like the lines of a hand, written in the corners of the streets, the gratings of the windows, the banisters of the steps, the antennae of the lightening rods, the poles of the flags, every segment marked in turn with scratches, indentations, scrolls."[2]

In making such subliminal connections, Knodel's work ranges across time and

traditions, ignoring conventional boundaries to commingle hybrid species and man-made forms. Clearly, the evolution of the work itself led him to mesh disparate disciplines, those that are the concern of textiles with those of painting, architecture and theater. He has been also an advocate in his work of the integration of various disciplines without a hierarchy, within the same curriculum.

Knodel apprenticed in the Western textile arts, having his roots in the theoretical geometry of Bauhaus textiles designed to fit into the modernist architecture of the 1920s and 1930s. During the 1970s, when the contemporary craft movement reached maturity, he welcomed the influx of fine arts ideas into textiles. The point was not to make textiles into paintings or architecture, or vice versa, but with painting to rethink the integration of three-dimensional imagery in the two-dimensional plane; or with architecture the relation of the two-dimensional image in the three dimensional volume. For instance, he brought the idea of the figure/ground composition of the medieval 'Lady and the Unicorn' tapestries into the late 20th century, using a post-modern conflation of divergent realities that was intentionally disjointing to interrupt the intrinsic beauty of textiles. In his tapestries from this period onward, space is no longer depicted as continuous, but fractured by the breaking up of the figure in the weft and the ground in the warp, creating conflicting flat or perspectival images—a highly innovative approach to the weaving process. The fact that the work is perceptually as well as conceptually based is obvious, for by lifting images off any ground plane, by making multiple horizons or horizonless spaces, he has made imagery contained only by boundaries that are set by the viewer's mind and eye. The imagery is also out of scale and in scale, is photographic and woven, depictive and realistic, executed in a variety of styles. Both representational and symbolic color is used in a single work, chosen to embody a sensation, a location or an abstract meaning. New materials, like reflective Mylar, are incorporated with natural fibers, as he experiments with shifts in perception and tactility to create linkages with recent technologies as well as with the commonalities of popular culture. Juxtaposing opposites within a single container is a seminal Knodel tactic.

In his architectural installations, Knodel continues the same practices, adding the experiential dimension of the viewer moving in and around a piece, defining and filling a space in various manners with the suspended textiles. In their interaction with the physicality of architecture, his installations move a space beyond its usual demeanor and into a post-modern engagement with the shifting, multiple

perspectives of many entry points both actual and conceptual, layered on top of the organizing geometry. The figure/ground relationship is also critical. According to architect and theorist Steven Holl, "Enmeshed experience, or the merging of object and field, is an elemental force of architecture."[3] By losing the separation between object and field, Knodel's installations become one with the space and the viewer moving within is confined in the composition. At the same time Knodel's extensive travels to non-Western societies led him to interweave in a work a complex succession of historic patterns and imagery inspired by the ethnographic textiles he collects. Rather than directly appropriating, he did what the Persians did to a naturalistic flowering tree pattern found in Indian textiles. They interpreted it within their own aesthetic. According to Knodel, the migration of meaning through cultural exchange via textiles is an important condition of his art. So too, the decorative qualities of patterning have been a sustained influence on his work.

In the more than 30 years he has been making art, his work has become dense with meaning. It has always been inclusive without being ponderous, beautiful without emphasizing beauty. These artistic traits are critical. Not only did he foresee some of the implications of human confinement within the global

village, he continually created the conceptual stage for experiencing the imagined consequences of it in a place where evolved natural and human forms first appear displaced, then reconnected, fused and finally, centered.

Knodel became artist-in-residence in the fiber department at Cranbrook Academy of Art in 1970. In the Cranbrook environment, an early 20th century utopian dream realized on Michigan farmland, he found support for his inventiveness, leading him to new ways of exploring the physicality of textiles. Originally, it was the theater that drew Knodel to the textile medium, and the theater has continued to be an influence. The fantasy conjured within a space made by the sets and the curtains, the anticipation at first, then the enduring aftermath: all of it was something he wanted to relate. He knew he had to work large and evoke in the viewer the intellectual and sensory triggers found within the space and time of dramatic experiences. Hence, with his earliest textile experiments he created interactive spaces. With '44 Panel Channel ' (1973), the textile equivalent of a minimalist grid-based sculpture, he hung rectangular fabric panels in chromatic sequences. The viewer could walk among the panels, Knodel explained, "with hands at your sides, through the narrow corridor of silk, wherein the experience becomes the

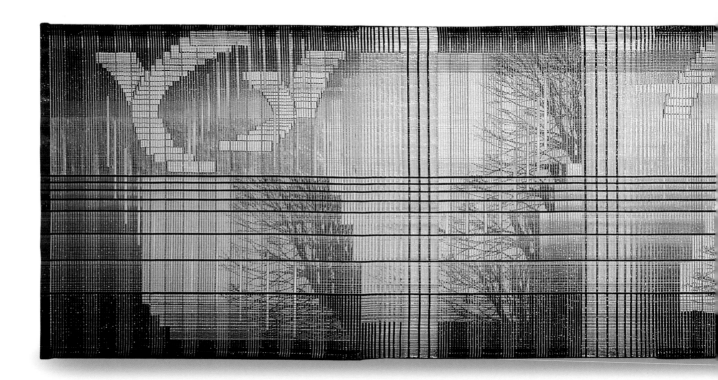

Second Nature

1986

cotton, mylar, rayon, linen

50 x 223in (125 x 557cm)

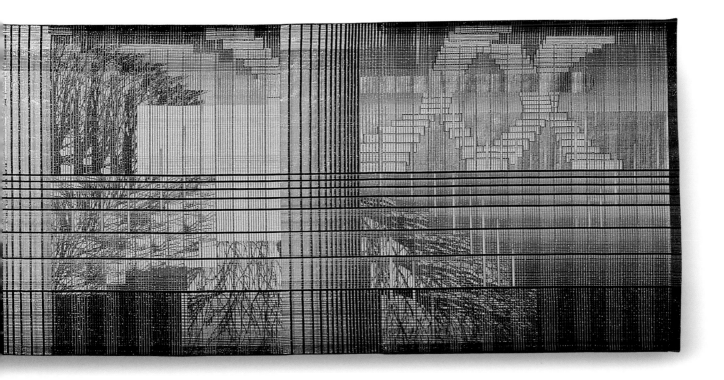

essence of the artwork."[4] Optically what happened was that as one moved the curtains parted, revealing the chromatic sequence from warm to cool in the light colored by the fabric, as well as the fabric, so the viewer experienced a spectrum. Then Knodel realized he could shape a freely floating textile in space using a grid of cords that pulled at it, acting much like strings on a marionette. The method enabled him to form the 'Parhelic Path' (1975), two dramatic curved floor-to-ceiling curtains that blocked off and created a new walled architectural space in the prestigious Lausanne International Biennale of 1975. Woven sections of yellow, blue, orange and silver Mylar cast a gorgeous colored light, appropriating architectural space within the aura of the piece. Here Knodel simultaneously shaped, and activated the space through the flexible panels. 'Free Fall' (1977), the first of his monumentally scaled installations, combined both earlier tactics, physically shaping and filling a space. Panels of hand-woven fabric in lush greens and yellows to cool purples and blues were draped from the ceiling to float downward like pages of a book, free of the binding. The panels moved with the air currents, bouncing light around and imparting energy and warmth to what had been a huge, overwhelmingly concrete atrium space. Permanently hung in a falling posture, the visual defiance of gravity's effects suspended certain

realities, creating a zone for contemplation. Art and architecture were combined to influence social interaction. During the 1980s, Knodel concentrated on adding dense content to his textile walls. 'Pontiac Curtain' (1982), a homage to Pontiac (the city in which he had a new studio), is part WPA mural, part hometown sampler and a portrait of a community balanced on the edge of past decay and future renewal. Photographic images of local people were transferred to the weft, then inserted into the warp "structured with color, line and light to build a field of atmosphere housing the figure,"[5] and merging figure with ground. A woven streetscape at the bottom recalled the early perspectival landscapes in Renaissance tapestries, conceptually exploring visually manipulated depth versus the constructed depth of the textile. Words lifted from buildings and sidewalk function as literal signs and as images. The work is a social document empowering the population with heightened awareness of the communal fabric.

With 'Guardians of the New Day' (1987), Knodel returned the power of an iconographic symbol, mainly from non-Western art, to his imagery, used here for his missive about ecological balance. Contemporarily dressed men, reproduced photographically, acted as guardians protecting the natural elements of land,

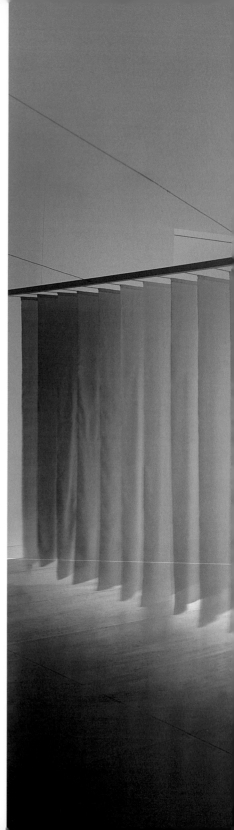

above:

Pontiac Curtain

1982

cotton, mylar, metal, linen

168 x 432 x 13in (420 x 1080 x 26cm)

page 26:

Guardians of the New Day

1987

cotton, linen, mylar

42 x 93 x 6in (105 x 232 x 15cm)

water, air and light, like characters out of a contemporary staging of a historic drama. In 'Guardians of a New Life' (1987), woven abstracted plant forms derived from Indonesian textiles are formally subverted to illustrate the hybridization of nature. With all these tapestries, Knodel used patterning to magnify the structure, making the layers visible from the loose scale of the basic gridded threads, to the repeated intersection of similar imagery. His point being, that all the parts of a piece count.

In the room-size installations, 'Bird Wall' (1989) about manipulation of the natural world, and 'Walls' (1991), of the relationship between the mind-body human container; large rectangular spaces are created by a manufactured netting that forms a transparent grid. Strips of fabric interlaced into the net created images that appeared to float. Knodel used the spatial element of cloth as a field that can be inhabited, seen into and through, loosening the language of space so it can be understood from a number of viewpoints. 'Walls,' a series of huge heads into which one walked to find frames where the viewer became the subject, provided an "existential experience of human kind as 'chambered beings existing only because of a flow of air, water and food through the spaces of our bodies, through the interstices of our being.' "[6] As we are trapped in our

bodies, so birds seeking freedom in the installation seemed to fly higher and higher within the space. " Birds are free to fly—nets entrap birds. My birds fly because of the nets which allow them to be free." [7] Knodel also continually questions where one finds art. "Can a wall be the embodiment of the architectural idea and be art that is normally thought to hang on it?" he asks. [8]

From 1993 on, the conceptual and literary meanings in the work grew more complex, as did Knodel's experimentation with materials and other artistic disciplines. A group of photographs and small sculptures (1993), acted as surrogates for text, some dealing with issues of the hand as a receptor of tactile knowledge, others the notion of pedagogy and the confinement or expansiveness of words—what the artist calls the elasticity of meaning. In part he was exploring how we come to know something, whether from history, experience or observation and the relationship of such knowledge. He was also shifting the prominence of elements, giving for instance, historical information or the experiential or the decorative more weight or less in particular pieces, to set up different conditions. Knodel says of these pieces: "They came into being as diagrams for understanding structures through the hand, taking you back through a simple place of intersection,

to discover something." [9]
A series of weavings based on palindromes took images from linked words to understand meanings that are present but overlooked, like the shadow that reveals much about a form, or the space inside the grid. With 'First Leaf/Leaving First' (1993), Knodel said he wanted to make something substantial out of leaves falling from the trees in fall. Similarly, 'Dawn's Promise' (1993), is a sumptuous curtain woven of metallic gimp. Simple in its form, it transformed a light-filled empty space with a textile that created the sensation of light, a golden light that almost dematerialized its architectural location.

With 'Nightshade' (1995), part of the exhibition 'Interventions,' at the Detroit Institute of Arts, Knodel made visible the relationship between the distant past and the present with his pierced textile mantle that projected images of contemporary Iranian life onto historic plates and vessels from ancient Persia contained in museum vitrines. By creating a context and some sense of change over time for what were isolated aesthetic objects, he expanded and enhanced meaning, as well as commented on museum objects separated from their cultural content. 'Lifelines' (1996), at Beaumont Hospital in Royal Oak, Michigan consists of 28 screens of off- white fiber spread across a 45' high by 100' long space, providing

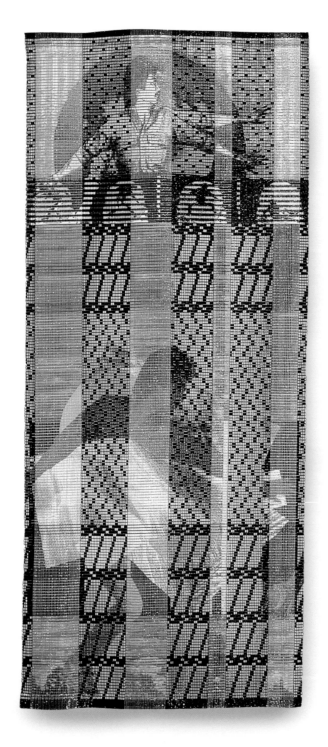
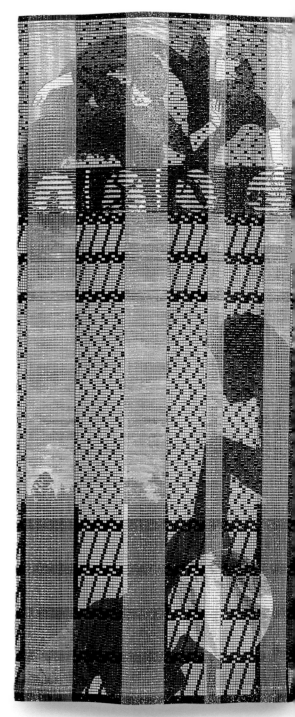

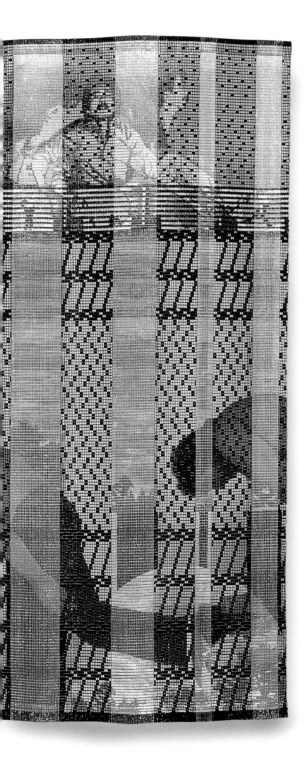

a privacy wall for patients in their rooms adjacent to an atrium. Cutwork text on the panels consists of phrases of healing taken from various cultures that appear like an incantation to be read; room to room and floor to floor. They fill the void of this cool modern space with interlinking references to the omnipresent yet ageless desire to be well. A commissioned piece for the 50-foot high central atrium of a public library in Northville, Michigan, 'Skydance at the Western Gate' (1998), turned the plethora of languages found in literature and on objects into metallic foil symbols. At the ceiling, fragmented letterforms are configured as if from an early language, spelling a word hidden among the cacophony. As the fragments descend into the space, nearer the viewer, they begin to organize in horizontal rows, like words in succession, to suggest more of our own language, recalling the way we expect to find words on the printed page. A metaphor for communication, the empathetic reaction clearly leads to the feeling that meaning is not easily accessible, that language, incipient in the early grunts and groans of man, is a communal response. Rather than a tower of Babel, this constellation of lighted shapes recalls the trial and error,

the challenges, that go into attempts to make meaning from experience. The point of this piece can be explained in part by an idea of Steven Holl's: "Language without sentences, just like natural light, has essences that transcend specific meanings and purposes." [10]

What Knodel has been seeking begins with textiles and ends with the human connection of individual experience with enduring commonalities. He says, "I am trying to find the patterns within experience. By revealing that which is known somatically, we trust in our biological being. The visual and experiential knowledge that accrues through a lifetime is primary knowledge that links people with fundamental cultural connections throughout time. I want to know how far distant something can be from me and still be related. If I touch a textile from Indonesia done 200 years ago by someone I didn't know, in a place I've never been, I still sense a linkage. The past rushes forward to the present with those connections and all that was formally distant and invisible is on the doorstep. Life is realized in recycled energy. A language of structure is a means of filtering that knowledge to give it tangible order." [11]

References

1. Gerhardt Knodel, 'Mysterious Voids at the Heart of Historic Textiles,' an introduction to an exhibit at The Textile Museum, Washington DC, early draft.
2. Italo Calvino, *Invisible Cities*, Harcourt Brace Jovanovich Publishers, New York, 1974, p10.
3. Steven Holl, *'Parallax,'* Princeton Architectural Press, New York, 2000, p56.
4. Conversation with the author, July 3, 2002.
5. Gerhardt Knodel, Letter to Jan van der Marck, July 22, 1998.
6. Vince Carducci, 'Gerhardt Knodel,' review with quote by Knodel in *The New Art Examiner*, February 1994, p39.
7. Laurel Reuter, 'Walls,' *American Craft Magazine*, October/November 1991, pp40-45.
8. Conversation with the author, June 13, 2002.
9. Ibid.
10. Holl, *'Parallax,'* p104.
11. Conversation with the author, July 3, 2002.

Skydance at the Western Gate
1998
metallic foil, synthetics
180 x 240 x 240in
(360 x 600 x 600cm)

Isola Bella
1990
45 x 54in (18 x 22cm)
private collection, Reading, Pennsylvania

Gerhardt Knodel: Portfolio

We knew what had been.
We know what was to come.
We believed in that which was on both sides,
but were without either.

A closet held two party dresses which she had worn.
She stood before them and remembered.

Meanwhile, Icarus put on his wings and
The conductor lifted his baton.

We were the space between.

Entre'acte
1983
cotton, wool, mylar, nylon,
theatrical scrim, velour
Museum of Fine Art,
Lausanne, Switzerland

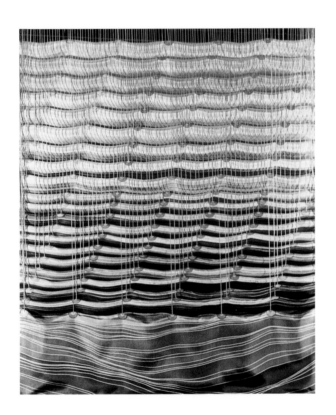

opposite:
Song of Songs
1995
architectural glass window and
printed fused glass suspended in
embroidered metallic curtain
144 x 240 x 96in
(360 x 600 x 240cm)

this page:
Seascape II
1974
silk, nylon, metal hardware
50 x 40 x 2in
(125 x 100 x 5cm)

above and opposite:

Night Shade

1995

mixed synthetics, photographic film
positives, existing Islamic decorative arts in
the collection of the Detroit Institute of Arts
60 x 192 x 192in (150 x 480 x 480cm)

*In 1995, the Detroit Institute of Arts created an exhibition
called 'Interventions', wherein a number of artists were
asked to create new work in relation to existing museum
collections. 'Night Shade' addresses the depletion of
meaning that art often suffers when placed in museums–
especially those works whose cultural context is foreign to
most visitors.*

*By covering a group of Islamic objects with a fabric 'tent',
'Night Shade' evoked the temporary nomadic architecture
of the Middle East. Viewers become voyeurs, gazing at
objects in the 'tent' through piercing in the fabric.*

*Inside, works of art that have been removed from their
original context find a more sympathetic environment than
the impersonal gallery. The fabric's metallic quality
suggests insulation from the cold and also conveys a
particular feeling of place and time.*

*The installation was an imaginative allusion to "a tent seen
at nightfall by a river on the Iranian plain." The silvery tent
evokes a distant moonlit night, the images printed on the
fabric lining situate the work in the contemporary world.*

G K

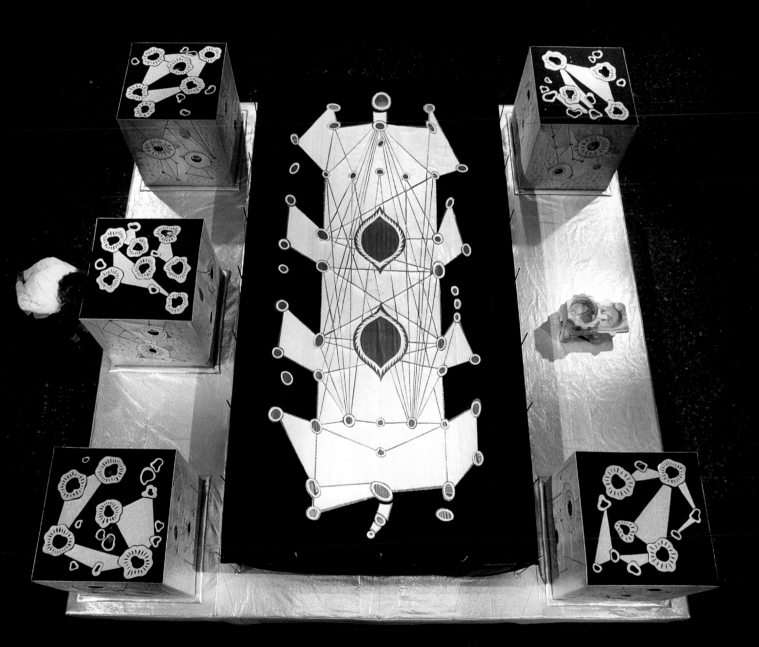

Relatively Yours
1997
polycarbonate, vinyl, metallic foil, mylar, light
108 x 240 x 480in (270 x 600 x 1200cm)
Installation for Mott Community College, Michigan

'Relatively Yours' includes four pairs of panels perforated with the names of individuals whose lives were separated by time and circumstances. These paired names form provocative relationships (for example Aretha Franklin and Benjamin Franklin). When the viewer enters the space between the panels, spotlights project the pairs of names onto the viewer's body. The viewer becomes the location for the meeting of two individuals. However, because they are projected onto opposite sides, they never can be seen simultaneously by the viewer.

G K

Lifelines

(detail, see also pages 42-43)

1996

PVC coated fiberglass, wool felt,

polypropylene net, metal armature

"Magic is when you will something into existence because you have need for it."
Black Elk

"You can't dance at two weddings at the same time; nor can you sit on two horses with one behind."
Jewish proverb

"The Quality of one's life depends on nothing but the mind."
The Dhammapada

"Natural forces within us are true healers."
Hippocrates

"Maintaining order rather than correcting disorder is the ultimate principle of wisdom."
The Nei Jing

"Rain beats on leopard skin but it does not wash out the spots."
Ashanti of Ghana

"Those who have health have hope and those who have hope have everything."
Arab proverb

A fabric wall comprised of 28 screens that capture changes in day or night light for patients whose rooms face on to the atrium.

Fragments of text on the subject of healing are accessible from each room, but the complete text is not.

Meaning is constructed slowly, like healing.

G K

Lifelines
1996
PVC coated fiberglass, wool felt,
polypropylene net, metal armature
540 x 1200x 36in (1350 x 3000 x 90cm)
Beaumont Hospital, Royal Oak, Michigan

43

Biography

Born	1940, Milwaukee, Wisconsin

Education and Awards

1961	University of California at Los Angeles, Bachelor of Arts
1970	California State University at Long Beach, Master of Arts
1976	National Endowment for the Arts, Visual Artist Fellowship
1984	Japan/United States Friendship Commission Fellowship
1988	Michigan Council for the Arts, Creative Artist Grant
1990	Distinguished Alumnus Award, California State University at Long Beach
1993	Honorary Fellow, American Craft Council, New York
1997	Honorary Doctorate, Maryland Institute, College of Art
2002	The Distinguished Craft Educators Award, Fiber, James Renwick Alliance Renwick Gallery of the Smithsonian American Art Museum, Washington

Professional

1970-95	Artist-in-Residence, Department of Fiber, Cranbrook Academy of Art
1996-present	Director, Cranbrook Academy of Art, Bloomfield Hills, Michigan

Selected Solo Exhibitions

1980	'Schoenbrunn Suite and Related Works,' The Hadler/Rodriguez Gallery, New York
1981	'Inside Out,' Philadelphia College of Art, Pennsylvania
1982	'Gerhardt Knodel Makes Places To Be,' Cranbrook Academy of Art Museum, Michigan
1984	'Gerhardt Knodel - New Work,' Elements Gallery, New York
1986	'Gerhardt Knodel,' Weatherspoon Art Gallery, University of North Carolina at Greensboro
1987	'Gerhardt Knodel - New Work,' Miller/Brown Gallery, San Francisco, California
1989	'Birds,' Yaw Gallery, Birmingham, Michigan
1990	'New Works by Gerhardt Knodel,' Textile Arts International, Minneapolis, Minnesota
1991	'Walls,' Seattle Pacific University, Washington
1993	'Gerhardt Knodel: Works in Fiber,' Dennos Museum of Art, Traverse City, Michigan
1995	'Deconstructed/Reconstructed,' Sybaris Gallery, Royal Oak, Michigan
1998	'Gerhardt Knodel - Skywalking,' Sybaris Gallery, Royal Oak, Michigan

Selected Group Exhibitions

1969   'New York: Young Americans 1969,' University of New Mexico, Museum of
Contemporary Crafts

1971   'California Design XI,' Pasadena Art Museum, California

1975   '7th Biennale Internationale de la Tapissierie,' Musée Cantonal des Beaux-Arts, Palais de
Rumine, Lausanne, Switzerland

1976   'Frontiers in Contemporary American Weaving,' Lowe Art Museum, University of Miami, Florida

1977   'Art Fabric,' The Allrich Gallery, San Francisco, California
'8th Biennale Internationale de la Tapissierie,' Musée Cantonal des Beaux-Arts,
Palais de Rumine, Lausanne, Switzerland
'Fiberworks,' Cleveland Museum of Art, Ohio

1978   'Diverse Directions: The Fiber Arts,' Museum of Art, Washington State University and
Henry Gallery, University of Washington

1979   'Art in Architecture,' Kemper Gallery, Kansas City Art Institute, Missouri

1980   'Across the Nation - Fine Art for Federal Buildings,' National Collection of Fine Arts, Washington, D.C

1981   'The Art Fabric: Mainstreams,' San Francisco Museum of Art, California
'4th Textile Triennale,' Central Museum of Textiles, Lodz, Poland

1983   '11th Biennale Internationale de la Tapissierie,' Musée Cantonal des Beaux-Arts, Palais
de Rumine, Lausanne, Switzerland

1985   '5th Textile Triennale,' Central Museum of Textiles, Lodz, Poland
'Cranbrook Contemporary,' Museum of Art, Sao Paulo, Brazil
'Poetry of the Physical,' American Craft Museum, New York

1987   'International Textile Competition,' Kyoto Conference Centre, Kyoto, Japan

1988   North Dakota Museum of Art: Frontiers in Fiber; The Americans,
'Contemporary Textiles; Traditional Roots,' Minneapolis Institute of Arts, Minnesota
'Grand Prix des Metiers D'Art,' Montreal, Quebec, Canada

1992   'International Contemporary Fiber Art Now,' Sonje Museum of Contemporary Art,
Kyong-ju, Korea

1994   'New Dyed and Printed Textiles: Japan and the USA,' Kyoto City Museum, Japan

1995   'Interventions', Detroit Institute of Arts, Detroit, Michigan
'Bridging Worlds: The Visiting Artists - Jacquard Project,' Paley Design Centre,
Philadelphia College of Textiles & Science, Pennsylvania

Selected Publications and Reviews

1981   Constantine, Mildren/Larsen, Jack Lenor, *The Art Fabric: Mainstream*, New York, Van Nostrand Reinhold

1982   Exhibition catalogue, *Gerhardt Knodel Makes Places To Be*, Cranbrook Academy of Art

1983   'Gerhardt Knodel Makes Places To Be,' pp97, 121-125, *American Craft*, February/March, pp. 30-31

1985   'Conversing with Gerhardt Knodel,' *Fiberarts*, January/February, pp27-31

1989   'The Lausanne Biennale: An Interview With Gerhardt Knodel' by Charles Talley,
        Surface Design Journal, pp14-21
        Shared Boundaries, The Cranbrook Tradition,
        Published by Craft Alliance Centre for the Visual Arts, St. Louis, Missouri

1990   'Gerhardt Knodel: Weaving a Textile Language' by Kathleen McCann. *Fiberarts*

1991   'Walls' by Laurel Reuter. *American Craft*, October/November

1992   'New Dialogues: Contemporary Fiber' by Margo Shermeta,
        Catalogue essay for Sonje Museum of Art, Seoul, Korea

1994   'Gerhardt Knodel' by Vincent Carducci, *New Art Examiner*, February

1995   'Rethinking Museums' by Glen Mannisto, *Detroit Metro Times*

1996   'Enter: Repeat' by Margo Mensing, Catalogue essay, 'Bridging Worlds' Exhibition,
        Philadelphia College of Textiles and Science
        'When the Community Joins In: The Recent Work of Gerhardt Knodel,' by Becky Hart,
        Fiberarts, September/October

1999   'Art and the American Experience,' Kalamazoo Institute of Arts, Kalamazoo, Michigan

Public Collections

National Museum of Fine Arts, Washington DC
Cranbrook Academy of Art
Minneapolis Institute of Art
Milwaukee Museum of Art
Detroit Institute of Arts
Rhode Island School of Design
Wadsworth Atheneum
Indianapolis Institute of Art

Other titles in this series

Vol 6: Anne Wilson
By Tim Porges and Hattie Gordon
ISBN 1 902015 22 3 (softback)

Vol 8: Helen Lancaster
ISBN 1 902015 29 0 (softback)
ISBN 1 902015 45 2 (hardback)

Vol 9: Kay Lawrence
ISBN 1 902015 28 2 (softback)
ISBN 1 902015 44 4 (hardback)

Vol 10: Joan Livingstone
ISBN 1 902015 27 4 (softback)
ISBN 1 902015 43 6 (hardback)

Vol 11: Marian Smit
ISBN 1 902015 32 0 (softback)
ISBN 1 902015 46 0 (hardback)

Vol 12: Tanaka Chiyoko
ISBN 1 902015 24 X (softback)
ISBN 1 902015 42 8 (hardback)

Vol 14: Lia Cook (Sept 02)
ISBN 1 902015 34 7 (softback)
ISBN 1 902015 51 7 (hardback)

Vol 15: Jane Lackey (Sept 02)
ISBN 1 902015 35 5 (softback)
ISBN 1 902015 52 5 (hardback)

Vol 16: Gerhardt Knodel (Sept 02)
ISBN 1 902015 47 9 (softback)
ISBN 1 902015 48 7 (hardback)

Vol 17: Kyoung Ae Cho (Feb 03)
ISBN 1 902015 35 5 (softback)
ISBN 1 902015 50 9 (hardback)

Vol 18: Jason Pollen (Feb 03)
ISBN 1 902015 73 8 (softback)
ISBN 1 902015 74 6 (hardback)

Vol 19: Barbara Layne (Feb 03)
ISBN 1 902015 36 3 (softback)
ISBN 1 902015 76 2 (hardback)

Vol 20: Kay Sekimachi (Feb 03)
ISBN 1 902015 77 0 (softback)
ISBN 1 902015 78 9 (hardback)

Vol 21: Emily DuBois (Feb 03)
ISBN 1 902015 38 X (softback)
ISBN 1 902015 54 1 (hardback)

Vol 22: Gyöngy Laky (Feb 03)
ISBN 1 902015 39 8 (softback)
ISBN 1 902015 56 8 (hardback)

Vol 23: Virginia Davis (Feb 03)
ISBN 1 902015 40 1 (softback)
ISBN 1 902015 57 6 (hardback)

Vol 24: Piper Shepard (Feb 03)
ISBN 1 902015 81 9 (softback)
ISBN 1 902015 82 7 (hardback)

Vol 25: Valerie Kirk (Feb 03)
ISBN 1 902015 37 1 (softback)
ISBN 1 902015 55 X (hardback)

Vol 26: Annet Couwenberg (Feb 03)
ISBN 1 902015 79 7 (softback)
ISBN 1 902015 80 0 (hardback)

Vol 27: Susan Lordi Marker (Feb 03)
ISBN 1 902015 41 X (softback)
ISBN 1 902015 58 4 (hardback)

Vol 28: Agano Machiko (Feb 03)
ISBN 1 902015 59 2 (softback)
ISBN 1 902015 60 6 (hardback)

Vol 29: Fukumoto Shihoko (Feb 03)
ISBN 1 902015 61 4 (softback)
ISBN 1 902015 62 2 (hardback)

Vol 30: Cynthia Schira (Feb 03)
ISBN 1 902015 63 0 (softback)
ISBN 1 902015 64 9 (hardback)

Vol 31: Kumai Kyoko (Sept 03)
ISBN 1 902015 65 7 (softback)
ISBN 1 902015 66 5 (hardback)

Vol 32: Suzie Brandt (Sept 03)
ISBN 1 902015 67 3 (softback)
ISBN 1 902015 68 1 (hardback)

Vol 33: Darrel Morris (Sept 03)
ISBN 1 902015 69 X (softback)
ISBN 1 902015 70 3 (hardback)

Vol 34: Pauline Burbidge (Feb 04)
ISBN 1 902015 71 1 (softback)
ISBN 1 902015 72 X (hardback)

Visit www.telos.net for further details